easy drum beats & fills

30 simple and fun beats to play on y...

Includes Online Audio, Video, and Metronome!

`T0085064`

PLAYBACK+
Speed • Pitch • Balance • Loop

To access audio, video, and extra content visit:
www.halleonard.com/mylibrary

Enter Code
3012-6984-4228-5870

ISBN 978-1-4950-9348-7

Copyright © 2018 by HAL LEONARD LLC
International Copyright Secured All Rights Reserved

Visit Hal Leonard Online at
www.halleonard.com

Contact Us:
Hal Leonard
7777 West Bluemound Road
Milwaukee, WI 53213
Email: info@halleonard.com

In Europe contact:
Hal Leonard Europe Limited
42 Wigmore Street
Marylebone, London, W1U 2RN
Email: info@halleonardeurope.com

In Australia contact:
Hal Leonard Australia Pty. Ltd.
4 Lentara Court
Cheltenham, Victoria, 3192 Australia
Email: info@halleonard.com.au

Contents

How to read music

Music is written with notes and rests. A **note** means to play; a **rest** means to rest (or pause). All notes and rests are written on a **staff**, which consists of five lines and four spaces. For drummers, each line and space represents a different drum or cymbal on the drumset. A symbol on the left side of the staff called a **percussion clef** tells you this is a staff for drums. Take a look below to see if you can identify where your different drums and cymbals are on the staff.

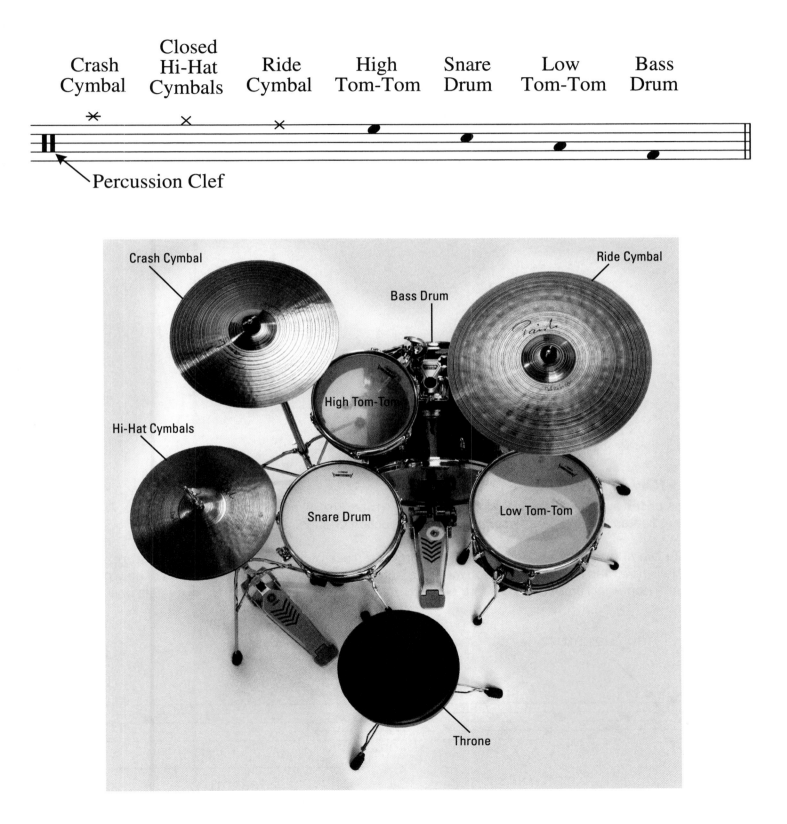

NOTES AND RESTS

Every note or rest has a rhythmic value. This tells you how long, or for how many **beats**, it will last:

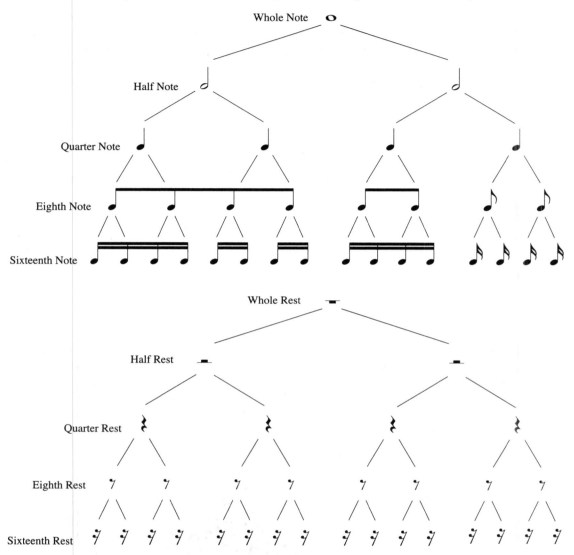

TIME SIGNATURES

Bar lines on the staff separate notes into measures. A **measure** is the space between bar lines. A **double bar line** indicates the end of a piece of music, or a section change.

There are two numbers that appear at the beginning of a piece of music called a **time signature**. The top number tells how many beats are in each measure and the bottom number tells what kind of note gets one beat. In 4/4 (four-four) time, there are four beats in each measure and the **quarter note** gets one beat.

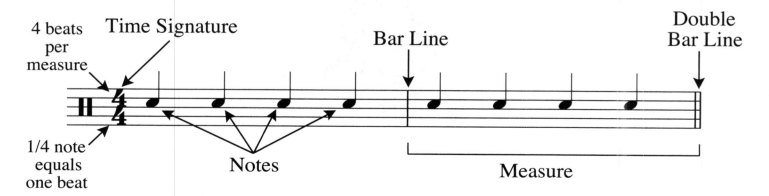

How to use this book

This book is designed to get you playing some great drum beats, which are all paired with several specifically designed drum fills. A "drum beat" is the general groove—the "meat and potatoes" of a song. A "drum fill" is a short break in the groove; it's a change that "fills in the gaps" of the music and/or signals the end of a phrase leading to another section of the song.

Typically, you'll end a drum fill with a crash cymbal and bass drum played together to begin the next section of a song. Most songs are composed of four-bar phrases. You'll play a beat for three measures and then play a drum fill for the fourth measure. This is a great way to practice all of these examples, and you'll get the feel of playing four-bar phases as you would in songs.

Here is an example:

For each audio track, you'll hear the primary beat played three times followed by the appropriate fill (A, B, or C). Every track will end with a crash cymbal and bass drum played together (on what would the fifth measure), although this is not notated. All of these drum beats can be played on either the hi-hat or the ride cymbal. Try both!

In addition to audio demonstrations for all the examples, this book also includes video performances of each beat and fill, plus a bonus online metronome to use for practicing! To access all of these features, simply visit **www.halleonard.com/mylibrary** and enter the code from page 1 of this book.

We've included the right- and left-hand sticking to indicate the best way to play these fills. If you are a left-handed drummer, just reverse these stickings. Good sticking choices help you to get around the drums most effectively without having to cross over with your hands.

All of these drum beats and fills are written to be played on a four-piece drumset (bass drum, snare drum, high tom, and low tom). If your set up includes more toms, you can use the same rhythms of these written fills and place the notes on different toms—or even the snare or bass drum. Keep in mind that a change of sticking may be required to easily get to a particular drum when adding extra toms. It's great practice having to think ahead and choose the best sticking on the fly. This may be difficult at first, but you'll get better with practice.

Some of the fills you'll play will be less than one full measure. In those cases, you'll just continue playing the drum beat up to when the fill begins. Sometimes you may end up altering the end of a drum beat to smoothly transition into a fill (just read the fills as written to understand).

You should also experiment with making up your own fills and/or mixing and matching parts of fills to form interesting combinations. Listen to recordings of your favorite songs and "steal" cool fills. This will also give you ideas for more of your own fills. Included with each beat are real song examples so you can hear the beats in context. Note that all of these beats could be played at any number of tempos, and you should practice them that way.

Let's begin!

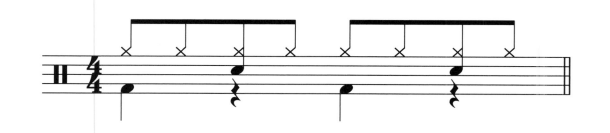

Fill A

Fill B

Fill C

Songs

Tom Petty: "Learning to Fly"
Michael Jackson: "Billie Jean"
Fleetwood Mac: "Dreams"

DRUM BEAT #2

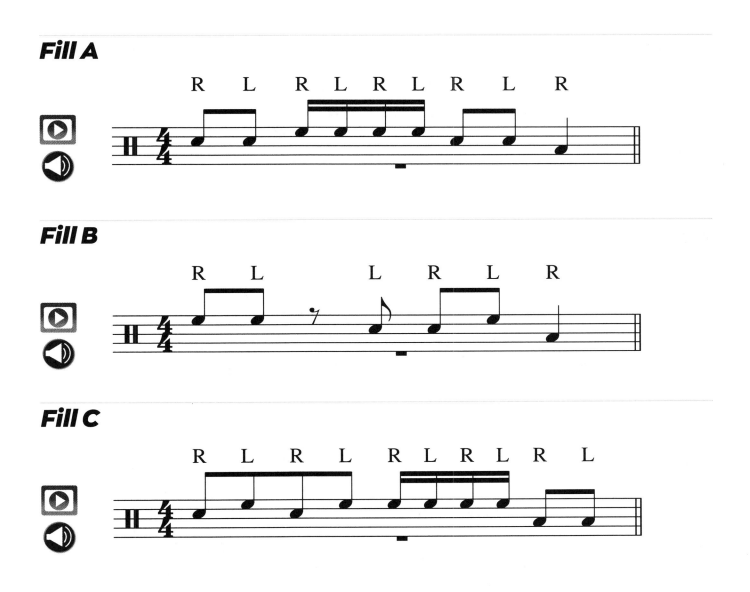

Fill A

Fill B

Fill C

Songs

The Clash: "Should I Stay or Should I Go"
The Beatles: "I Want to Hold Your Hand"
Eagles: "New Kid in Town"
Creedence Clearwater Revival: "Have You Ever Seen the Rain?"

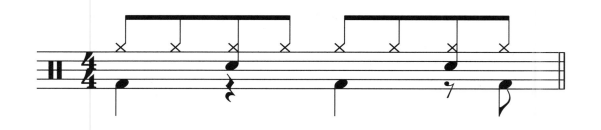

Fill A

Fill B

Fill C

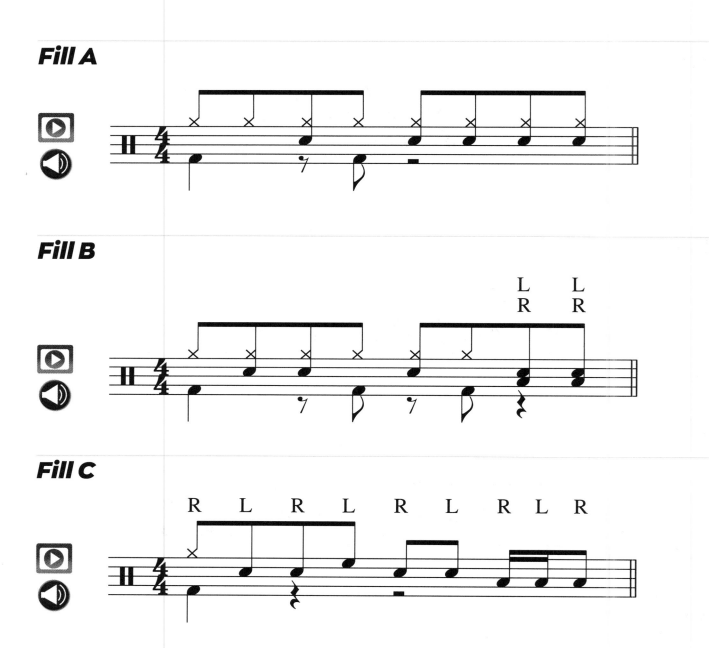

Songs

John Mellencamp: "Hurts So Good"
The Doors: "Light My Fire"

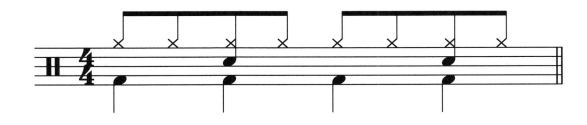

Fill A

Fill B

Fill C

Songs

Queen: "Another One Bites the Dust"
Bob Seger: "Old Time Rock & Roll"
Stevie Wonder: "Living for the City"

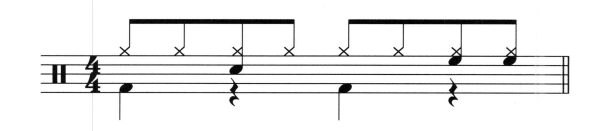

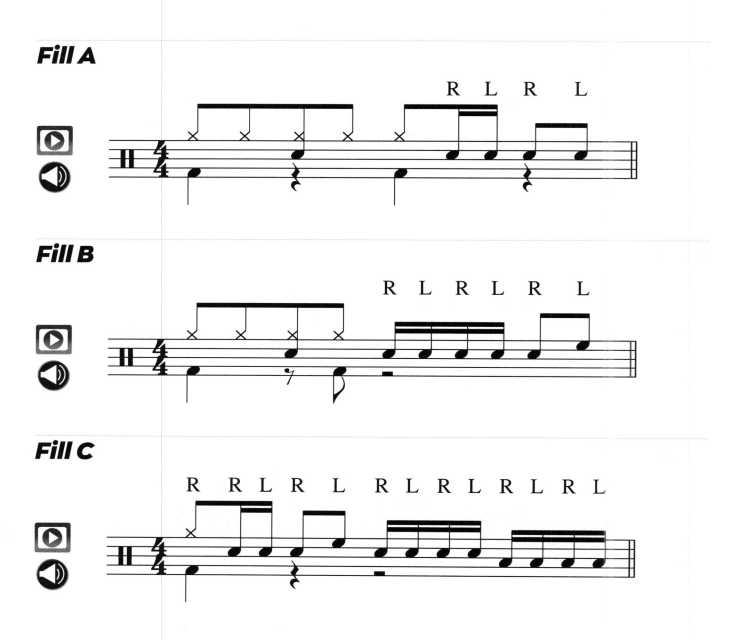

Fill A

Fill B

Fill C

Songs

Barrett Strong: "Money (That's What I Want)"
John Mayall & the Bluesbreakers: "All Your Love (I Miss Loving)"

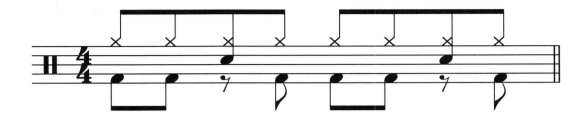

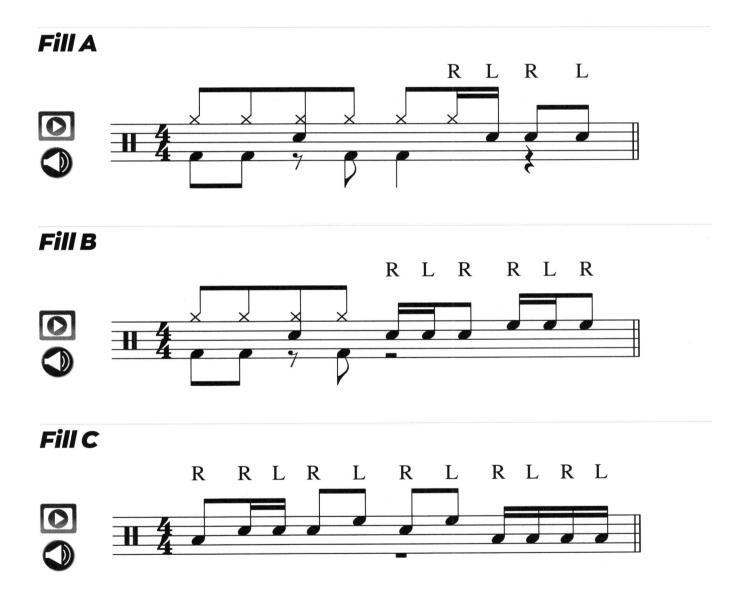

Fill A

Fill B

Fill C

Songs

Blue Öyster Cult: "Don't Fear the Reaper"
Creedence Clearwater Revival: "Fortunate Son"

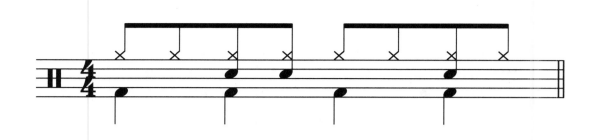

Fill A

Fill B

Fill C

Songs

The Beach Boys: "Surfin' U.S.A."
Del Shannon: "Runaway"

Fill A

Fill B

Fill C

Songs

Tommy James and the Shondells: "Mony Mony"
Kiss: "Rock and Roll All Nite"
Aerosmith: "Back in the Saddle"
Fleetwood Mac: "Rhiannon"

DRUM BEAT #9

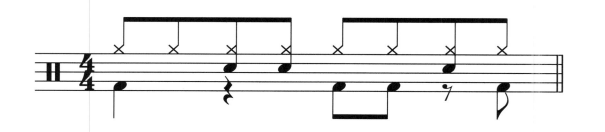

Fill A

Fill B

Fill C

Songs

The Contours: "Do You Love Me"
The Marvelettes: "Please Mr. Postman"

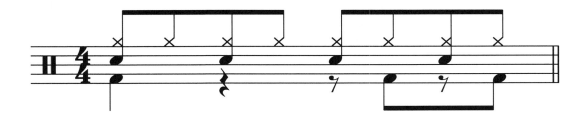

Fill A

Fill B

Fill C

Songs

Four Tops: "I Can't Help Myself (Sugar Pie Honey Bunch)"
The Jimi Hendrix Experience: "Purple Haze"
Stevie Wonder: "Uptight (Everything's Alright)"

DRUM BEAT #11

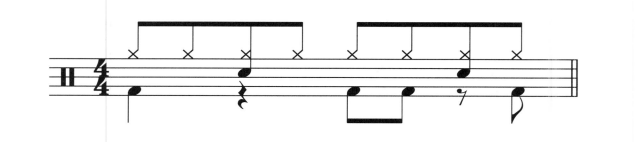

Fill A

R L R L R

Fill B

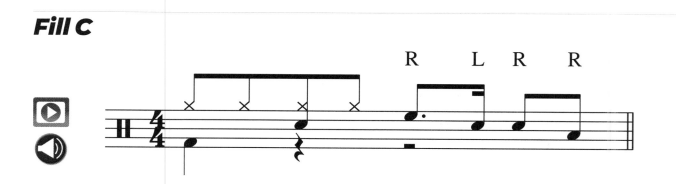

R R L R L R L R L R R

Fill C

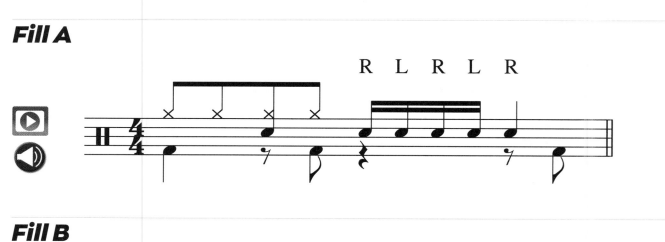

R L R R

Songs

Martha and the Vandellas: "Dancing in the Street"
The Temptations: "My Girl"
Marvin Gaye and Tammi Terrell: "Ain't No Mountain High Enough"
Steely Dan: "My Old School"

A great way to make a drum sound bigger and fatter is to play a **flam**. The flam consists of a **grace note** and a **main note**. The grace note is played softer and just before the main note. Start by holding your left stick about three inches above the head and your right stick ten inches. As you bring both sticks toward the head, the left should hit first (grace note), followed by the right (main note).

Grace note →   ← Main note
L R

This is called a **right flam**. The flam is named after the main note. To play a left flam, simply reverse the sticking. The notes should be played close enough together so they sound as one note, but not exactly at the same time or they will produce what is called a "flat" flam.

On the next page, you'll see some flams used in the examples. Let's try them out!

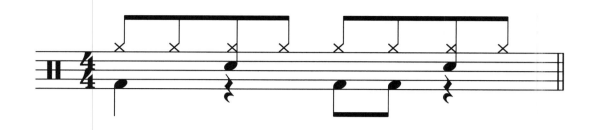

Fill A

Fill B

Fill C

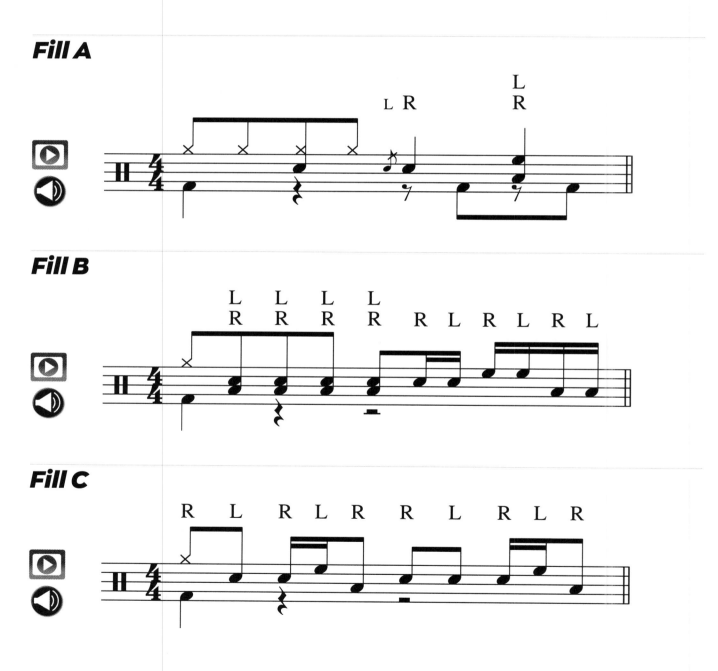

Songs

Judas Priest: "Living After Midnight"
Green Day: "21 Guns"
The Beatles: "Back in the U.S.S.R."
Wilson Pickett: "In the Midnight Hour"

Fill A

Fill B

Fill C

Songs

The Beatles: "Day Tripper"
Tom Petty: "You Don't Know How It Feels"
Aerosmith: "Back in the Saddle"
Weezer: "Beverly Hills"

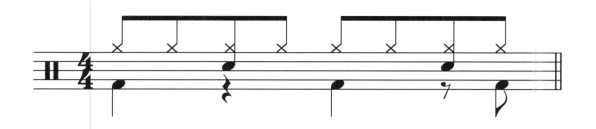

Fill A

Fill B

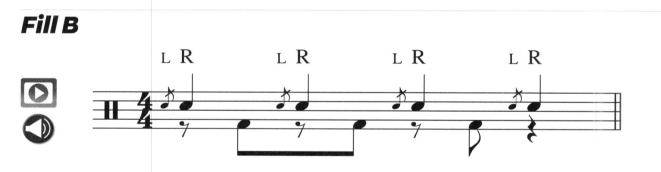

Fill C

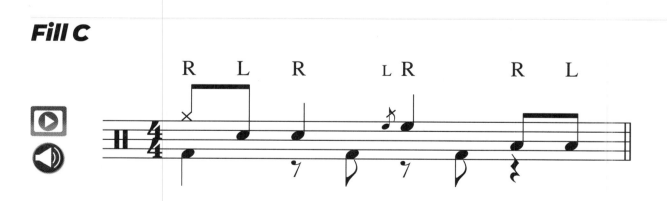

Songs

AC/DC: "Highway to Hell"
The Rolling Stones: "Tumbling Dice"

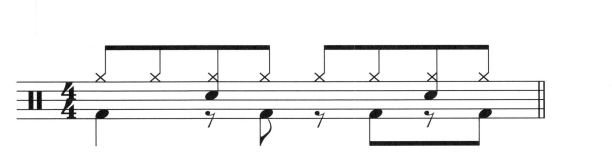

Songs

War: "Low Rider"
Cheap Trick: "Surrender"

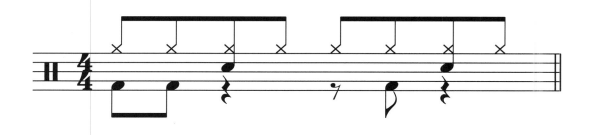

Fill A

Fill B

Fill C

Songs

The Kingsmen: "Louie Louie"
Scorpions: "Rock You Like a Hurricane"

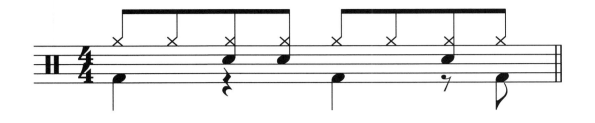

Fill A

Fill B

Fill C

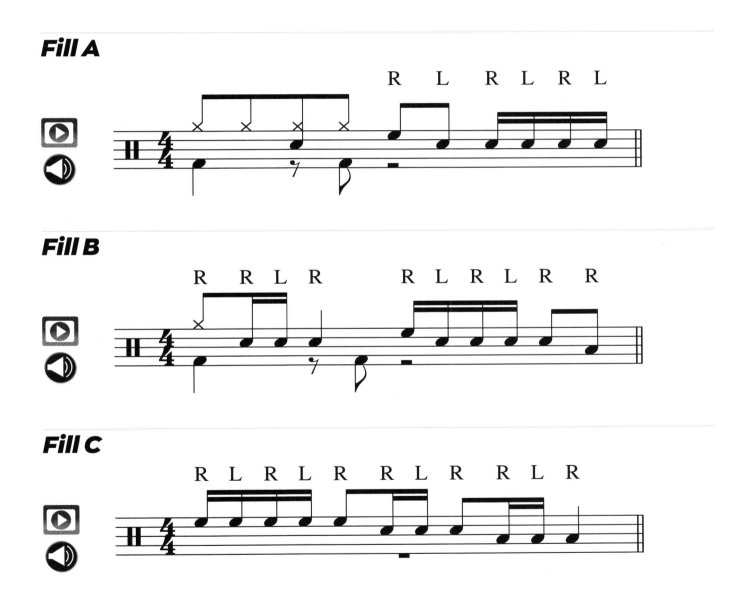

Songs

The Beatles: "Twist and Shout"
The Doors: "Hello, I Love You"

Fill A

Fill B

Fill C

Songs

The Rolling Stones: "Beast of Burden"
Nirvana: "About a Girl"
Santana: "Smooth"
Rick James: "Super Freak"

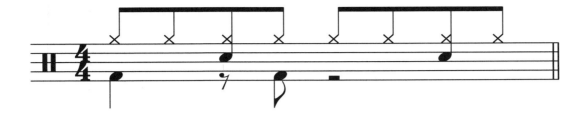

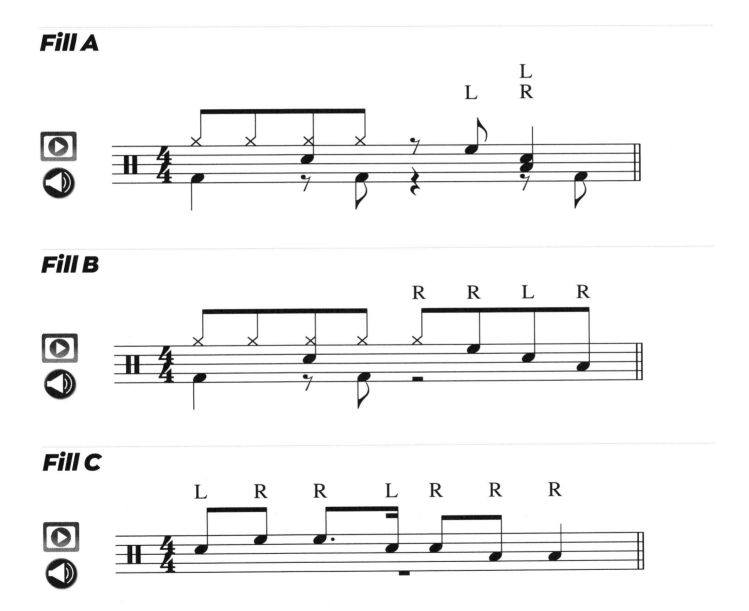

Fill A

Fill B

Fill C

Songs

Tom Petty and the Heartbreakers: "Don't Do Me Like That"
George Benson: "On Broadway"

Fill A

Fill B

Fill C

Boston: "Rock and Roll Band"
Weezer: "Say It Ain't So"
Scorpions: "No One Like You"

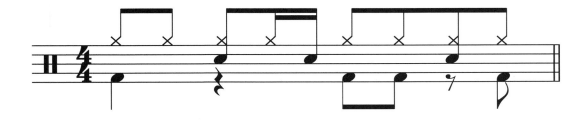

Fill A

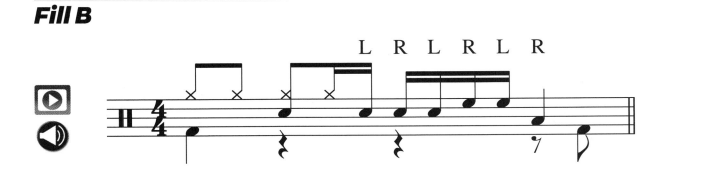

Fill B

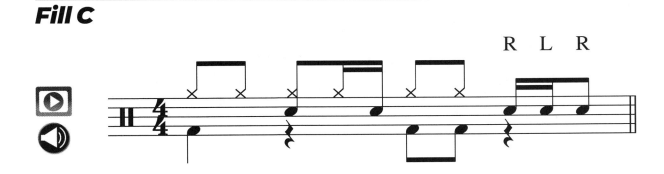

Fill C

Songs
Aretha Franklin: "Respect"
Sam & Dave: "Soul Man"
Albert King: "Born Under a Bad Sign"

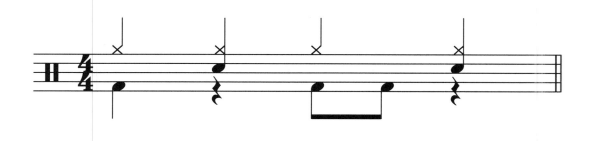

Fill A

Fill B

Fill C

Songs

Free: "All Right Now"
Tom Petty and the Heartbreakers: "I Need to Know"
Bachman-Turner Overdrive: "Takin' Care of Business"
Rod Stewart: "Maggie May"

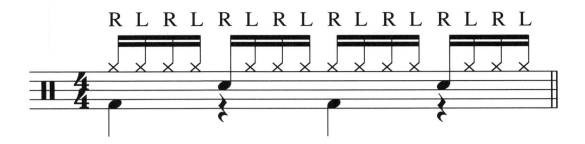

Fill A

Fill B

Fill C

Songs

Deep Purple: "Smoke on the Water"
Foo Fighters: "Everlong"

Fill A

Fill B

Fill C

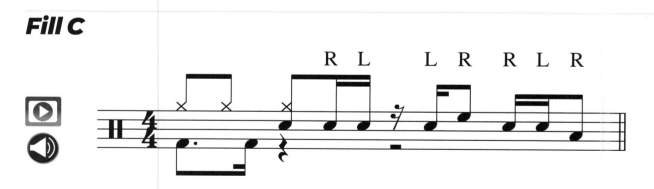

Songs

Pearl Jam: "Even Flow"
Weezer: "Say It Ain't So"
Matchbox 20: "3 am"

Fill A

Fill B

Fill C

Songs

Cream: "White Room"
Sam & Dave: "Hold On, I'm Comin'"

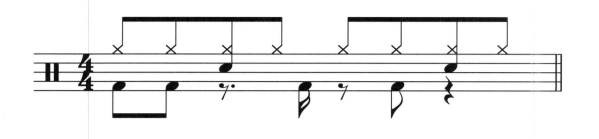

Fill A

Fill B

Fill C

Songs

Stone Temple Pilots: "Plush"
Incubus: "Drive"
Red Hot Chili Peppers: "Aeroplane"

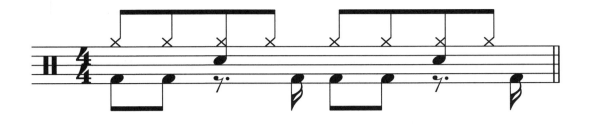

Fill A

Fill B

Fill C

Songs

Bad Company: "Shooting Star"
The Isley Brothers: "It's Your Thing"

DRUM BEAT #28

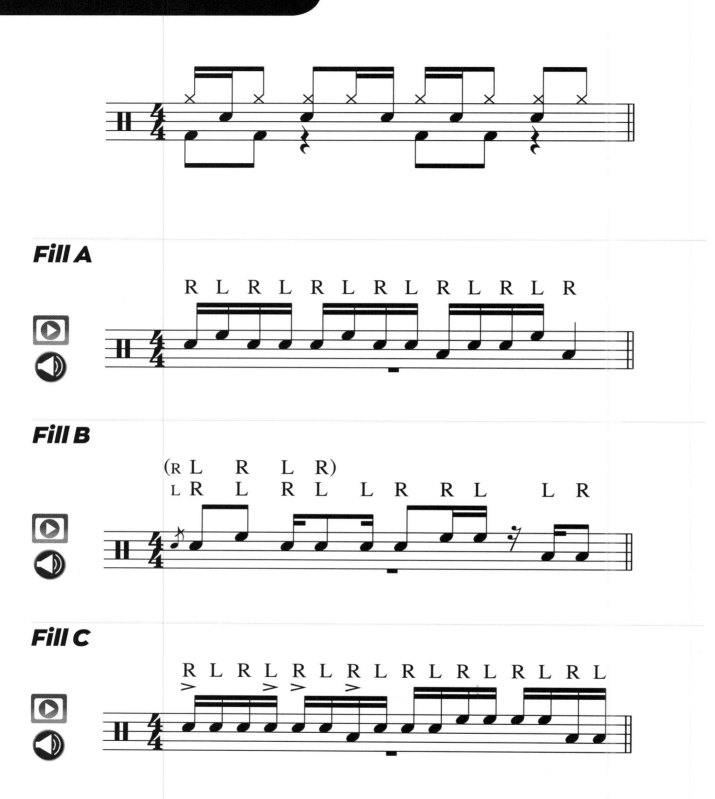

Fill A

Fill B

Fill C

Songs

Stevie Wonder: "For Once in My Life"
The Jimi Hendrix Experience: "Fire"

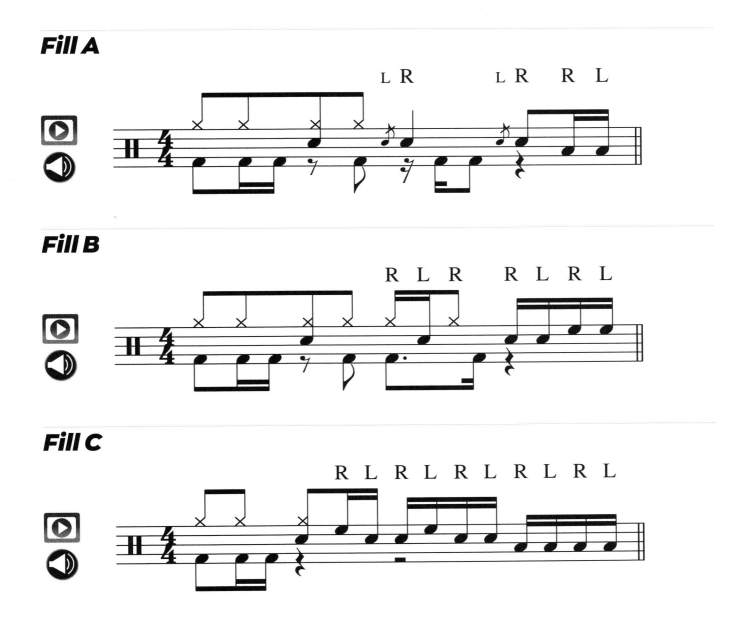

Fill A

Fill B

Fill C

Songs

Johnny Winter: "Rock Me Baby"
Black Sabbath: "N.I.B."

Fill A

Fill B

Fill C

Songs

Rage Against the Machine: "Know Your Enemy"
Gov't Mule: "Steppin' Lightly"

YOU CAN'T BEAT OUR DRUM BOOKS!

Learn to Play the Drumset – Book 1
by Peter Magadini
This unique method starts students out on the entire drumset and teaches them the basics in the shortest amount of time. Book 1 covers basic 4- and 5-piece set-ups, grips and sticks, reading and improvisation, coordination of hands and feet, and features a variety of contemporary and basic rhythm patterns with exercise breakdowns for each.
06620030 Book/CD Pack.. $14.99

Creative Timekeeping for the Contemporary Jazz Drummer
by Rick Mattingly
Combining a variety of jazz ride cymbal patterns with coordination and reading exercises, *Creative Timekeeping* develops true independence: the ability to play any rhythm on the ride cymbal while playing any rhythm on the snare and bass drums. It provides a variety of jazz ride cymbal patterns as well as coordination and reading exercises that can be played along with them. Five chapters: Ride Cymbal Patterns; Coordination Patterns and Reading; Combination Patterns and Reading; Applications; and Cymbal Reading.
06621764 .... $9.99

The Drumset Musician – 2nd Edition
by Rod Morgenstein and Rick Mattingly
Containing hundreds of practical, usable beats and fills, The Drumset Musician teaches you how to apply a variety of patterns and grooves to the actual performance of songs. The accompanying online audio includes demos as well as 18 play-along tracks covering a wide range of rock, blues and pop styles, with detailed instructions on how to create exciting, solid drum parts.
00268369 Book/Online Audio $19.99

Drum Aerobics
by Andy Ziker
A 52-week, one-exercise-per-day workout program for developing, improving, and maintaining drum technique. Players of all levels – beginners to advanced – will increase their speed, coordination, dexterity and accuracy. The online audio contains all 365 workout licks, plus play-along grooves in styles including rock, blues, jazz, heavy metal, reggae, funk, calypso, bossa nova, march, mambo, New Orleans 2nd Line, and lots more!
06620137 Book/Online Audio $19.99

40 Intermediate Snare Drum Solos
For Concert Performance
by Ben Hans
This book provides the advancing percussionist with interesting solo material in all musical styles. It is designed as a lesson supplement, or as performance material for recitals and solo competitions. Includes: 40 intermediate snare drum solos presented in easy-to-read notation; a music glossary; Percussive Arts Society rudiment chart; suggested sticking, dynamics and articulation markings; and much more!
06620067 .... $7.99

Joe Porcaro's Drumset Method – Groovin' with Rudiments
Patterns Applied to Rock, Jazz & Latin Drumset
by Joe Porcaro
Master teacher Joe Porcaro presents rudiments at the drumset in this sensational new edition of *Groovin' with Rudiments*. This book is chock full of exciting drum grooves, sticking patterns, fills, polyrhythmic adaptations, odd meters, and fantastic solo ideas in jazz, rock, and Latin feels. The enclosed CD features 99 audio clip examples in many styles to round out this true collection of superb drumming material for every serious drumset performer.
06620129 Book/CD Pack $24.99

Show Drumming
The Essential Guide to Playing Drumset for Live Shows and Musicals
by Ed Shaughnessy and Clem DeRosa
Who better to teach you than "America's Premier Showdrummer" himself, Mr. Ed Shaughnessy! Features: a step-by-step walk-through of a simulated show; CD with music, comments & tips from Ed; notated examples; practical tips; advice on instruments; a special accessories section with photos; and more!
06620080 Book/CD Pack $16.95

Instant Guide to Drum Grooves
The Essential Reference for the Working Drummer
by Maria Martinez
Become a more versatile drumset player! From traditional Dixieland to cutting-edge hip-hop, Instant Guide to Drum Grooves is a handy source featuring 100 patterns that will prepare working drummers for the stylistic variety of modern gigs. The book includes essential beats and grooves in such styles as: jazz, shuffle, country, rock, funk, New Orleans, reggae, calypso, Brazilian and Latin.
06620056 Book/CD Pack.. $10.99

The Complete Drumset Rudiments
by Peter Magadini
Use your imagination to incorporate these rudimental etudes into new patterns that you can apply to the drumset or tom toms as you develop your hand technique with the Snare Drum Rudiments, your hand and foot technique with the Drumset Rudiments and your polyrhythmic technique with the Polyrhythm Rudiments. Adopt them all into your own creative expressions based on ideas you come up with while practicing.
06620016 Book/CD Pack.. $14.95

Drum Dictionary
An A-Z Guide to Tips, Techniques & Much More
by Ed Roscetti
Take your playing from ordinary to extraordinary in this all-encompassing book/audio package for drummers. You'll receive valuable tips on performing, recording, the music business, instruments and equipment, beats, fills, soloing techniques, care and maintenance, and more. Styles such as rock, jazz, hip-hop, and Latin are represented through demonstrations of authentic grooves and instruments appropriate for each genre.
00244646 Book/Online Audio $19.99

Prices, contents, and availability subject to change without notice.

HAL•LEONARD®
www.halleonard.com
0818
022

HAL·LEONARD® DRUM PLAY-ALONG

Play your favorite songs quickly and easily with the *Drum Play-Along*™ series. Just follow the drum notation, listen to the CD or online audio to hear how the drums should sound, then play along using the separate backing tracks. The lyrics are also included for quick reference. The audio CD is playable on any CD player. For PC and Mac computer users, the CD is enhanced so you can adjust the recording to any tempo without changing the pitch!

1. Pop/Rock
00699742.................................$14.99

2. Classic Rock
00699741.................................$15.99

3. Hard Rock
00699743.................................$15.99

4. Modern Rock
00699744.................................$15.99

5. Funk
00699745.................................$15.99

6. '90s Rock
00699746.................................$17.99

7. Punk Rock
00699747.................................$14.99

8. '80s Rock
00699832.................................$15.99

9. Cover Band Hits
00211599.................................$16.99

10. blink-182
00699834.................................$16.99

11. Jimi Hendrix Experience: Smash Hits
00699835.................................$16.95

12. The Police
00700268.................................$16.99

13. Steely Dan
00700202.................................$16.99

15. The Beatles
00256656.................................$16.99

16. Blues
00700272.................................$16.99

17. Nirvana
00700273.................................$15.99

18. Motown
00700274.................................$15.99

19. Rock Band: Modern Rock Edition
00700707.................................$17.99

20. Rock Band: Classic Rock Edition
00700708.................................$14.95

21. Weezer
00700959.................................$14.99

22. Black Sabbath
00701190.................................$16.99

23. The Who
00701191.................................$16.99

24. Pink Floyd – Dark Side of the Moon
00701612.................................$14.99

25. Bob Marley
00701703.................................$14.99

26. Aerosmith
00701887.................................$15.99

27. Modern Worship
00701921.................................$16.99

28. Avenged Sevenfold
00702388.................................$17.99

30. Dream Theater
00111942.................................$24.99

31. Red Hot Chili Peppers
00702992.................................$19.99

32. Songs for Beginners
00704204.................................$14.99

33. James Brown
00117422.................................$16.99

34. U2
00124470.................................$16.99

35. Buddy Rich
00124640.................................$19.99

36. Wipe Out & 7 Other Fun Songs
00125341.................................$16.99

37. Slayer
00139861.................................$17.99

38. Eagles
00143920.................................$16.99

39. Kiss
00143937.................................$16.99

40. Stevie Ray Vaughan
00146155.................................$16.99

41. Rock Songs for Kids
00148113.................................$14.99

42. Easy Rock Songs
00148143.................................$14.99

45. Bon Jovi
00200891.................................$16.99

46. Mötley Crüe
00200892.................................$16.99

47. Metallica: 1983-1988
00234340.................................$19.99

48. Metallica: 1991-2016
00234341.................................$19.99

49. Top Rock Hits
00256655.................................$16.99

Prices, contents and availability subject to change without notice and may vary outside the US.

Visit Hal Leonard Online at
www.halleonard.com